Answers to Life's Questions

OTHER BOOKS BY JOHN-ROGER

Blessings Of Light
Divine Essence
Dream Voyages
Forgiveness – The Key To The Kingdom
Fulfilling Your Spiritual Promise
God Is Your Partner
Inner Worlds of Meditation
Journey Of A Soul
Loving Each Day
Loving Each Day For Moms & Dads
Loving Each Day For Peacemakers
Manual On Using The Light
Momentum: Letting Love Lead (with Paul Kaye)
Passage Into Spirit
Psychic Protection
Relationships: Love, Marriage & Spirit
Sex, Spirit & You
Spiritual High
Spiritual Warrior: The Art Of Spiritual Living
The Consciousness Of Soul
The Path To Mastership
The Power Within You
The Rest of Your Life (with Paul Kaye)
The Spiritual Family
The Spiritual Promise
Walking With The Lord
The Way Out
Wealth & Higher Consciousness
What's It Like Being You? (with Paul Kaye)
When Are You Coming Home? (with Pauli Sanderson)

For further information, please contact:
MSIA, P.O. Box 513935, Los Angeles, CA 90051
323-737-4055
soul@msia.org www.msia.org

Q&A
ANSWERS TO LIFE'S QUESTIONS

JOHN-ROGER, DSS

MANDEVILLE PRESS
Los Angeles, CA 90051-1935

Copyright © 2000
Peace Theological Seminary & College of Philosophy

All rights reserved, including the right of reproduction
in whole or in part in any form.

Published by Mandeville Press
P.O. Box 513935
Los Angeles, California 90051-1935
(323) 737-4055
jrbooks@msia.org

Printed in the United States of America
I.S.B.N. 1-893020-07-X

Visit us on the Web at www.mandevillepress.org

Introduction

For over thirty years, John-Roger has been answering questions about Soul transcendence, the spiritual nature of life, and practical spirituality. We hope you enjoy reading this small but profound and engaging sample of questions and answers from that thirty-year period. It covers a wide spectrum of subjects, and I am sure you will find questions here that you have often asked, such as, "What is the meaning of Life?" Well, yes, that question is answered here—and if you have ever wondered whether your cat is more spiritual than you are or whether it's better to be an angel, that too is addressed.

At some point in the future, we plan to provide an extended version of this book, covering more subjects with many more questions and answers. Until then, we leave you with this gem of a book to give you food for thought and nourishment for your spirit.

Paul Kaye
President
MSIA

Angels

*Q: What is the difference between a human Soul
and an angel?*

A: An angel comes from the devic kingdom, which is a specialized form of comfort and service. The human Soul is a branch off God itself. Angels worship the Soul because, while in the physical body, they have come to serve mankind—and to bring comfort and joy.

*Q: Do people have guardian angels?
If so, what level do they come from
and what is their effect on us?*

A: If a person has been baptized through the "church," there is often a form which has been called a "guardian angel" placed with him at that time. The level that the form comes from would be, of course, the same level from which the energy of the church functions.

Guardian angels can be effective. The more a person works with them, the more effective they become. But you should never give yourself over to any entity form whatsoever. You can listen, take caution, question it, and check it, and for your own sake, test it—not give in to it. Test everything you hear, check it out. If it can't be proven or if it doesn't work for you, let it go. And don't hassle yourself that someone else seems to be doing "better" than you. Forget it; their way is not yours. The guardian angel is one who will urge and direct; it works like sort of a reflective counselor. When you work with it, it can be effective.

Animals

Q: What is the difference between animal and human Souls?

A: Generally speaking, humans have individualized Souls that are rather "high up" on the evolutionary scale. Animals, for the most part, have group auras. In other words, they are working in a mass consciousness of the species and are fulfilling their evolutionary progression in that way. Some cats (mostly Siamese), and occasionally some dogs may have an individualized Soul; and those are the ones that might come in as a basic self to a human consciousness in the next step of their progression. They are getting close to moving out of the "animal" category and into the "human" evolutionary process.

Q: Are animals here to evoke some emotion from us or teach us love?

A: Animals certainly do that a lot of the time, but that is not their primary function. They are here to express life.

ATTITUDE

Q: What is the difference between judging someone and telling them that they are stepping on my toes?

A: The difference is not in what you do, but in your attitude as you do it. It is possible for you to give someone the information that what they are doing is not working for you with an attitude of openness and neutrality.

What happens too often is that we do not speak up right away, and the energy of feeling imposed upon builds up until, by the time you get around to saying something, it comes out like an explosion. You have probably created anger, resentment and judgment around the situation by then, which comes across in your communication. Then you may feel guilty, thinking that it was what you said that was the problem when it was the build-up of emotional energy that most likely caused reaction in the other person.

As you learn to speak up in the moment something is going on, you may find that it becomes more and more easy to take care of yourself without moving into judgment of others or of situations. Watch your attitude; that is the key. For more information, you may want to listen to the seminar, "Letting the Energy Flow," or "How Can Negative Patterns Be Changed?"

Q: Sometimes I look back on some of the things I have done and wonder if I really needed that lesson. I did learn, but might there be another way?

A: In the Lord's Prayer (which is really the disciples' prayer), the disciples ask Jesus, "Lord, how do we pray?" And Jesus answers, "You pray this way: Our Father, who art in heaven..." That's the disciples' prayer. "Lead us not into temptation. Deliver us from evil."

Evil is unnecessary experience, so therefore evil is based back inside of us as, "I just didn't need that experience." Well, maybe you had that experience not for you, but for someone else. Years later someone may come up to you and you share what you know. They express their gratitude to you because it solved something for them.

And you find yourself saying inside, Thank God I had that experience, so I could assist this other person.

But maybe you consider robbing a bank. You could learn from the bank robbers who go to prison—so that might be an unnecessary experience, an evil, for you.

Do the best you can in each moment. It is also important to forgive yourself if you find yourself judging something that you have done. Use as much wisdom and loving as you can before you do things; then learn from what you do, and forgive anything that you are not happy with in your experience. Then you can start walking with the Lord.

Aura

Q: I hear people using the word "aura" but I don't really know what they're talking about except in a vague way. What is an aura?

A: The aura is a force field of electromagnetic energy that surrounds the body. When a person is healthy and balanced, his aura reflects his condition as being smooth and all parts being alive with clear color and free movement. If a person is experiencing disturbance, it is reflected in the aura. We all have auras, but not everyone can "see" auras. Some people sense them more than see them. For instance, have you ever walked into a room and encountered a person who you just don't want to be around because you sense something is not quite right? You are probably "sensing" their aura.

Q: Does our behavior or emotional state affect our aura?

A: Some types of human behavior have a direct effect on the aura, which then has a direct effect on the feelings of the person involved. Drugs, as one example, damage the aura. Because of the nature of the drug experience, definite changes happen to the person, his perception of his environment, his feelings, his responses, etc. Taking drugs often causes great irregularities in the aura, may cause rips and tears to appear, as the energy around the body is really blasted by the force of the drugs. Also, physical illness will be reflected in the aura—things as commonplace as a headache or as serious as pneumonia will show up in the aura. Many times a weakness in the auric force field will indicate a high potential for illness or injury in the area of the weakness. If the aura can be brought into balance, the physical manifestation of the weakness may be avoided.

Q: Are children's auras the same as adult's or do they change?

A: The physical aura will change; the mental aura will change; the spiritual aura will stay the same, for the most part. Children can have beautiful auras—so refined and pure. A little baby has such a perfected aura that you can't help but pick them up and love them, trying to drink in the purity of that child. They just radiate this Light and if you don't know what it is, you'll feel it as so much love. Mothers and fathers can tell you this.

AWARENESS & UNDERSTANDING

Q: There are so many things that I don't understand about myself and the world. It seems overwhelming. Where do I start?

A: Start with your next breath ... and take one step at a time. If you look at yourself and there seems to be many things that you would like to change but it's so overwhelming, you might not ever start. So start with one thing. And when you have succeeded with that one thing, you may decide to take on the next thing. Everything doesn't have to be changed overnight. Be patient with yourself, keep loving yourself and give yourself credit for the steps you are taking.

The same can hold true when you look at the "state of the world." If we look at all the things we would like to change, it might look overwhelming. Start with yourself. Bring yourself into line first—one step at a time. Taking care of yourself or changing yourself could have profound effects on the rest of the world. But remember also, that you are not responsible to change the entire world. Your main responsibility is to yourself.

*Q: I don't understand life at all.
Is there any meaning to any of this?*

A: You don't need to understand anything. But you may want to accept that you are here and have chosen this and can use your time here to lift yourself as high as you want. In the Movement of Spiritual Inner Awareness we teach many tools to assist you. But you must use and apply them to your life in order to have the results.

The nature of this planet is negative and it's sometimes easy to "fall asleep" and forget why you are here. The only thing you have to do while you're here is to awaken to the sound of God within your heart and follow that sound back to the heart of God.

JOHN-ROGER

Q: What is the meaning of life?

A: To know God personally.

Q: So much of my trouble seems to come from lack of awareness, but how do I get awareness in an area if I don't even know I'm unaware in it?

A: I think a lot of us could answer to that one. If we had all the awareness we wanted, we just wouldn't do a lot of the things that we do. But we probably wouldn't be here, either. It's important to remember "intention." God is your partner, and what you ask for is brought to you, although not necessarily in your timing, or looking the way you thought it would. So ask for greater awareness where you need it, for the highest good, and then watch. I have talked about keeping a journal, and this is another area in which you might do that. Keep track of awarenesses you have during the day, during your s.e.'s, or when you wake up in the morning. If you are watching and listening, you will realize when your awareness is awakening in a new way. Be grateful for what and who comes your way, and keep doing your spiritual exercises. These can also open the door to greater awareness.

Q: I have been very aware of God and the Light's presence with me when I needed help. What I would like is to be more aware of God when things are going well. Can you talk about that a little?

A: Our job is to keep practicing awareness, becoming aware. So when things are in balance, don't use that as a key to split off and daydream. Use that as a key to stay and enjoy what's present. As you do that, you can uncover things that might be pushing on you. As you keep your focus on being present, you can let go of the inner distractions by noting them but not focusing on them, or if it is something you need to handle, writing it down or going and handling it. All the while, you continue keeping your focus on the present. Are you getting that being present is part of being aware of the Lord?

BABIES & YOUNG CHILDREN

Q: I have a two-year-old child who wakes up in the middle of the night screaming and crying. She is really irritating me, as I feel it is just a game with her to get my attention and keep me from getting a good night's sleep. How can I work with her and myself?

A: Perhaps you are not giving her the attention she requires during the day. Have you taken the time to listen to her, to hold her, to really be with her during the day? Also, a technique to use is that after she is asleep, find a quiet place for yourself and silently ask her basic self to come and sit on your lap. You can love her and stroke her and ask her to tell you why she is upset and why she is crying at night. It is a very good technique to use. You can also communicate to her while she is awake and even though she doesn't yet have the vocabulary to express how she feels to you, she will communicate in her own way what is wrong. Children are amazingly open and willing to cooperate, but if you try to force them to do something your way, they will let you know in no uncertain terms that it's not the way they want to be treated. Be sensitive to her needs and also communicate your needs to her and see if you can find a way to cooperate with each other.

Q: Why are there so many cesarean births?

A: I don't know what "so many" means to you. If it is a comparative statement, I have no data indicating an increase or decrease in this medical action. Either way, cesarean or "natural," the child will come in if that is the Soul's intention. And since a Soul embodies, then I would not make a cesarean birth wrong, any better or worse than what we call "natural." The point of the action is that a Soul comes in. That is time to rejoice.

BALANCE

Q: You speak about keeping the physical, emotional and mental levels balanced. But you also say that what we do on this level does not affect the Traveler. Can you explain this?

A: As long as you want the Traveler to work with you, it will continue to work with you. If your emotions are out of balance, your mind is scattered or your physical body full of disease, the Traveler Consciousness will work with you to awaken you to your divine heritage. But you would be further ahead if you took full advantage of being in this physical body by taking care of it, nurturing it and loving it. And you may want to discipline your mind so your thoughts are directed toward God. And if you keep your emotions balanced, you can feel good about all those other things. Why not have the best of all things possible while you are here? The Traveler's work with you is in the Soul and that is independent of your physical, emotional or mental activities.

Baptism & Initiation

Q: *What is the purpose of baptism? How does that differ from the process of initiation?*

A: The purpose of baptism is to release the "sins" of this and previous lives and to receive a guardian angel who will work with you and assist you in your progression towards spiritual awareness. The ritual is primarily for the basic self and is symbolic of washing away past "sins" and bringing all levels into agreement and cooperation with Spirit. The process of initiation connects you to the fullness of your true self. I call it Soul Transcendence.

Q: *I was baptized about six years ago. Would there be any value in being baptized again? How does baptism assist a person in their spiritual growth?*

A: If you were baptized within MSIA, there is no value in being baptized again. Baptism is a ritual invoking the basic self to participate within the protection of the Christ, and a guardian angel.

CHAKRAS

Q: What's the relationship between the crown chakra, the Soul, and the high self?

A: I'll give you the answer by way of an analogy: the Soul is the director. The high self is the executive secretary. And the crown chakra is the office building.

Q: If the lower chakras of the body are open and there is a sincere desire to close those lower areas, how does one go about that?

A: Generally, to close the lower, sexual chakra areas of the body, you would turn your attention, your focus, and your energies up to the higher centers, specifically the third eye area or the crown chakra. You would chant the sacred names of God and direct your creative energy into Spirit, spiritual love, and service. The changes will not happen overnight, but they will happen. You may have spent many years being aware of the lower centers. So be prepared that it may take some time for you to reverse this process and become more totally attuned to your higher centers.

Christ—Jesus the Christ

Q: What is the relationship of Jesus the Christ who lived two thousand years ago to the Christ Consciousness that is here today?

A: We all have access to the Christ Consciousness today because the Christ said this was possible. And as soon as you say, "I believe," you're halfway there. The other half is to demonstrate it.

Prior to the time that Jesus entered into the sacrifice, the negative powers confined man to the lower realms of Light. Man was confined into the physical, causal, astral, mental, and etheric realms; he could not get back into the Soul realm, back to God. The cosmic mirror, which divides the etheric and Soul realms, always reflected man back into the lower realms so that he kept reincarnating back. Jesus came through from pure Spirit and bridged from the positive into the negative. In this bridging, he came down into the negative realms and told the negative forces that any human consciousness on any of these lower levels who turns towards God and Light and purity cannot be denied that turn and that movement. The Bible says it in different words; it says that Jesus unshackled, that he started the resurrection—not just of the physical, but of the whole, total process. This is why he is like one of the great hinges on the door of this dispensation into which we are moving. Buddha was also a hinge on the door, as was Moses and Abraham and many others. But I look at Jesus as being the top hinge. However, without all the other hinges on the door, Jesus' work would have been fruitless. We are also hinges on the door; we're also the door and the bridge on the other side of the door and we get to walk across the bridge. That's our job in this time. We chose it, every one of us. The key is to do it.

Q: What is the difference between "Christ Consciousness" and "cosmic consciousness"?

A: "Christ Consciousness" is a Christian way of saying "cosmic consciousness." To say, "Christ Consciousness" does not include the Buddhists, Moslems, etc. "cosmic consciousness" includes all people. But the two terms are so close in the level of consciousness they identify that there is almost no difference.

Q: What's the specific difference between the salvation of the Christ and Soul Transcendence as taught by the Traveler?

A: Jesus, through his death and resurrection, changed the karma of the planet. Before Jesus' time, the law of the planet was "an eye for an eye and a tooth for a tooth"—also known as the law of Moses. Through the Christ action, human beings came under grace, and salvation was won for all of us at that time. Through grace, our individual karma can be instantaneously dissolved; then we are no longer bound by the law of cause and effect in that area, providing we stay in the grace and do not recreate the karma. We open to grace by connecting to the Christ Consciousness within, thus becoming, in a sense, our own salvation.

Soul Transcendence, as taught by the Travelers (and Jesus was also a Traveler), is a process of balancing past actions on each of the levels (physical, astral, causal, mental, and etheric) and moving in consciousness into the Soul. Another way of saying it is that a person becomes aware of his or her Soul and, more than that, of being a Soul. As you can see, salvation through the Christ and Soul Transcendence are closely interwoven, although they are viewed as separate actions.

Q: I am Jewish and I am comfortable in believing that Jesus, like all of us, is the Son of God. I believe he, like Moses, played an important role in human growth towards the awareness of God. Jesus is God because we are all God and he is no more God than I am. Does this conflict with the views MSIA teaches and will my belief be a possible block in my path toward God or Soul awareness?

A: Your beliefs will not block your path to God and there is no conflict with what MSIA teaches and your perceptions. Your present perceptions can be amplified and expanded by saying we all have within us the potential to actualize our God or Christ self. Jesus reached his potential and manifested the Christ more fully than anyone had done at that time. He became the example many of us chose to follow because he represented the God-Man.

COLOR

Q: Sometimes I see flashes of purple, and I'm wondering if you would tell me what that means?

A: That purple is a specific energy field. It's a transmuting field, no matter how it appears. When you see the purple dealing with a person, one of first things it tells you is something's being transmuted, changed. And so it's a signal: "Go for it!" And you just let go and get rid of as much as you can. It may be transmuting for the other person, or you, or both of you.

Often when you see this purple, it means be aware. For example, you might see purple flash across the road when you are driving. Some people think wow, everything's fine; I can speed. That's the signal that there's a traffic cop up ahead and you're to be careful! So when it appears, one thing it is telling you is to be aware. Not beware, Be Aware. Something is going on. It may be for you, and it may be against you, but be aware.

Death & Dying

Q: Is the transition after death an innately beautiful process?

A: For those who are active initiates of the Traveler—meaning they are doing the spiritual exercises and working within the consciousness of the Traveler—the transition from this level can be a beautiful experience. The initiates are under the Traveler's protection; when an initiate passes over, they are taken by the Traveler to the appropriate level for them before the negative power even knows they have made their transition.

What can you do with this information? As always, use it for your advancement. Do your spiritual exercises and work with the Light as best you know how; check out the teachings and practice what works for you. Your transition will be part of God's plan for you and your awareness of what is going on at that time will be a result of the awareness you have created through your spiritual practices while you are living on this level.

Q: When someone I care for dies, how can I best support them spiritually?

A: Often the people closest to someone who is making their transition get caught up in the emotions and have a difficult time holding the Light clearly. A good thing to do is to call other ministers or initiates and ask them to hold the Light for all of the people involved—the individual making the transition and the people close to them.

There is a natural grieving process that goes on when someone you care for leaves this earthly plane. They are going to a far greater place. Those left behind need to deal with their sense of loss, and there are many ways to do this. A good suggestion would be to do free-form writing on a regular basis, giving you a place to express all the emotions and thoughts connected with the person who has died. You can also write to me, and either burn or mail the letter. As you write the letter, you are allowing me to work with you on the spiritual levels, and I do what I can to assist. Burning (or mailing) the letter helps you release it from your consciousness. Physical activity is also helpful, and doing service can assist you by allowing you an avenue through which your loving and caring for others can flow.

Decisions/Dilemmas

Q: When I have decisions to make and I try to make them with the Light, how do I know I've made the right decision?

A: In the Light, there are no "wrong" decisions.

Q: Then how would I make a decision—an answer that I know would be for my highest good?

A: Sometimes when you ask a question, when you ask God for an answer, and you ask "for your highest good," you won't get an answer—because that is for your highest good. Your spiritual teachers want you to work through patterns a little bit more, a little longer, to gain some more experience, rather than opening the door and ushering you out of the situation. It's important to remember that what is positive from the spiritual point of view may not appear to be positive from the physical point of view. But when you honestly ask "for your highest good" your experiences will be for your highest good.

Q: I find that I often come across situations where I have trouble making decisions. Can you suggest a technique that might make this process easier?

A: One technique that may work is to "mock up" seeing through the eyes of a master. You can call in the Light, asking for perfect protection, and then go inside and ask what the master would do in this situation. You may find that the answers come, and may be much more than just your own imagination. Then you can lean into what you have heard inwardly, and if it works for you, use it.

Q: I have a really difficult decision to make. And I just don't know which way to turn. Any decision I think of making seems wrong. It's really tearing me up. Can you suggest anything?

A: Take a good, long, hard look at all your choices that are available to you right now. Write them all down. Even write down the ones that you find unacceptable for some reason. Then by each possibility write down the "pros" and "cons," and run it out over several years' time, if necessary. When you get it all down on paper, you'll have it much clearer than it is right now, when it's all muddled up in your head. When you get it down on paper, look at it all, and make your decision from your intellect, not from your emotions, your desires, or your hurts, etc.—just from your intellect through observation.

Sometimes when you have made a "bad" choice and gotten yourself in a difficult situation, another "bad" choice has to be made to get you out of that. So keep in mind that none of your choices may appear to be "good" ones right now. But if you look at all the possibilities as clearly as you can and make your decision from your intellect, that will be all you can expect of yourself.

Desires

Q: I get confused about "asking for what I want." If God already knows all my needs, then it seems I shouldn't ask for anything. But the Bible also says, "You receive not because you ask not." Can you help me to understand this better?

A: When you are entering into a more spiritual consciousness, you'll find that before you can ask, your needs are already taken care of. Your wants and your desires are usually your problem areas. Do you know the differences between these? I'll illustrate here with a story. A man walked into a store to buy something, and the clerk came up to him and said, "Sir, what do you desire?" He said, "To kiss Rita Hayworth." She said, "Sir, I mean, what do you want?" He said, "A new Cadillac." She said, "Well, what do you need?" He said, "Some galoshes."

Most people's confusion comes in the area of their desires, not their needs. Giving can be one of the greatest ways to receiving. If you want more love, give love. If you want more joy, be joyful. Look for the good in all things and situations, and you may be surprised at what you see.

DISCIPLINE

Q: How do I develop discipline when I don't have any?

A: Discipline is not a possession to have or lose. Discipline is an expression that is developed by commitment and practice. I suggest you start slowly and set up a program for success. For instance, when a particular friend started doing spiritual exercises, he did only 10 to 20 minutes at each sitting. Then after a month of that, he set his timer to 25 minutes for a month; and then 30 minutes, etc. He took his time in going for the discipline, and over a period of time, this person now does 2 hours of spiritual exercises in one sitting. It isn't always easy, but who said it's supposed to be easy? There is an enormous value in discipline—the least amount of which is an inner knowing that you are the master of your fate rather than some addiction running you.

DIVINE PROTECTION

Q: When you state "dishonesty forfeits divine protection," how does that work out on the inner realms? I always thought it applied on earthly actions.

A: The way I have said it is that "dishonesty forfeits divine aid."

We are co-creators with God. If you are not honest with yourself, you are not being honest with God and not allowing God to come to your aid. This applies on the spiritual levels (inner and outer), and it filters into the physical level. Put another way, if you are not honest with yourself, you are keeping God out of that part of you that you are being dishonest about. God says, "Sure, if you want to keep me out of there, that's fine with me. I'm in no rush." And God lets you have what you indicate you want—that thing you are protecting, that thing you don't want to admit to yourself, that thing you probably really would like to let go of because it is a pain and an agony to you. And, often, as soon as you are honest with yourself about it—and that means you just acknowledge, "Yes, that's there in me"—this allows it to start to move because you are no longer denying its existence.

Doubt

Q: I have a lot of doubt about things. Can you help me?

A: My job is not to remove doubt. If I don't create doubt for you, then I haven't served you. Your doubt can become a tool for inquiry and your inquiry needs to be critical. Not negative, critical. That means looking very closely and precisely at something instead of just running your doubt as information or evidence. Doubt has no information or evidence in it. It has a feeling that things don't fit. You then use your intelligence to go in and see how they fit, or see what doesn't fit. When you are done, you will have proven something for yourself which no one can take from you, and that is very valuable.

Q: I have so much doubt that it's hard for me to believe in anything. I want to believe that s.e.'s are doing some good, but I just can't seem to get past my doubt. What can I do to change this?

A: To thine own self be true. You've got the result of entertaining doubt and you're not happy with it. Often when people doubt so much, they are really looking for the truth. They want to know the truth, and know that they know. Truth resides in us as the foundation of giving and living and sharing. Do you understand that you have to start giving in order to have what you're looking for? You have to expand beyond the doubting process, beyond your thinking process of doubt. You can do this by choosing to feel good and letting that good flood through your mind as joy.

A good way to get that feeling started is through being of service. And we're not looking for perfection here, we're just looking for the doing—from the excellence, the loving that's inside of you. Let the Spirit that is inside of you bring forward the perfection of you, for it knows much better than the rationality of the mind, or the emotions, or the body.

Choose you this day whom you serve. If you're serving in the house of God, you become a servant who's free. If you choose to serve in the house of doubt, then you're also the one who will slave to make sure the doubt maintains itself. It really is your choice.

Q: When one is traveling through the inner realms of Light, in the dream state, will the dreams appear as a colorform?

A: They could, but most of the time the dreams will come back into your physical memory as "stories." The basic self screens the "dream" experiences and brings them back to you in ways you can relate to readily. You might remember a dream of Soul traveling as driving up a hill in a car—that's "travel" as you understand it on the physical plane. Or you might remember getting on an airplane and flying somewhere, but you don't remember where. Or you might remember being with a group of people at a seminar. It may not have happened that way in the spiritual state, but you have to have some way to relate it to your physical experience. The storyteller inside of you will translate the spiritual experiences into physical symbols.

Q: Can you recommend any reading material that will help with the interpretation of dreams?

A: In general, dream interpretation is only accurate and only valid when done by the dreamer and not by any outside source. You are the only one who can accurately know what your dreams mean to you. If you tune in to your dreams, write them down, review them later in the light of what has taken place in your life since the time of the dream, etc., the interpretations will become clear to you. The more you do this, the more in tune with the process you become, and you will be able to interpret your dreams more quickly and accurately.

My book on dreams[1] has information about the various levels of dreaming, and you might find it helpful.

Q: I've been having a lot of bad dreams at night. When I wake up, I'm really frightened and sometimes shaking, and it can take hours to get myself back into balance and to sleep again. Can you suggest anything?

A: The dreams could be all sorts of things: clearing karma, releasing all sorts of stuff in the dream state, working through unconscious or subconscious fears, blocks, etc. You're your best interpreter of dreams. Whatever they are, though, don't give them a lot of power. If you wake up after a bad dream, just go to work with yourself. Chant the HU or the ANI HU. Surround yourself with

---

1. *Dream Voyages* by John-Roger is available in bookstores and through MSIA, P.O. Box 513935, Los Angeles, CA 90051, (323) 737-4055.

Answers to Life's Questions

the Light. Ask for the Mystical Traveler to help you release the dream experience. Keep some water by your bed and drink a little of it to break the intensity of the dream experience and to help you come back into the physical focus. There is also a tone of "E" that you can chant which will help to bring you back into physical focus. You just chant or say "eeeeeeeeeee"—a long, drawn out sound; you start the sound low, take it up as high as you can, then drop it back down as low as you can. That will help to bring you back solidly into the physical level. Also, exercise can break the unbalanced feeling from "bad dreams."

> Q: *What does tracking my dreams have to do with my spiritual exercises, or more to the point, my spiritual awareness and progression?*

A: There are many forms of spiritual exercises. It's a state of forcing yourself to be aware. If you go to sleep by midnight, and then wake yourself at 2:30 in the morning, there is a chance that you will be closer in contact with that other level that knows the dreams, and you could be pulling those across because there is less confusion in the mind.

If you want to find out where you are in your levels of spirituality, keep track of what you dream about. That will tell you where you are. Generally speaking, if you are dreaming about sex, food, your job, your spouse, or any number of material concerns, you will be incarnating back to those levels. Regardless of the level of initiation you have reached, you are going to pull yourself back to this level. Some of you dream with the Traveler, moving into other levels of consciousness and working things out. You are bringing balance to past actions. You are involved in it and you know it. Your awareness of this process lets you see your level of progression.

Q: Is there a way that I can become more attuned to the Christ Consciousness through my dreams?

A: Ask. As you go to sleep at night, you can ask that you be more attuned to that consciousness of the Christ. You can also ask that the Traveler work with you in whatever way is for your highest good and that you remember that which is beneficial for you to remember, in a way that you can understand. Then, when you wake up, you write down your dreams, or your sense of what went on in the dream state. Use all of this for your advancement. You can really set yourself up for success in having greater and greater awareness of the inner realms, and all of it can lead you to awareness of your Soul and the Soul realm, if that is what you want and where you want to go.

Drugs & Alcohol

Q: What's the difference between smoking dope or taking some form of drugs, and drinking alcohol?

A: It's sort of like drugs are a .38 and alcohol is a .45. They'll both kill you. The only difference is that alcohol goes out of the aura and out of the system faster. Drugs have an accumulating effect.

Drugs hang in the aura. Alcohol doesn't. I've seen people who may have smoked one joint of marijuana a year ago and I can still see the effects of that in their aura. It's still there after long periods of time. And it will still affect that person. But someone could have been very, very drunk two or three weeks ago, and I'll not be able to see that in the aura at all. I could see it if I were to go into Soul Consciousness and backtrack through their experiences, but I couldn't see it just by observing the aura. That's the difference that I can observe.

Earth Changes

Q: We have heard and read about the end of the millennium, the possible earth changes, and surely at least a major change in consciousness. How do we prepare spiritually and physically for the inevitable change in consciousness individually and for the human race en masse? And how should we prepare for possible earth changes? Do we ignore it physically move our families, wait and see?

A: There are always earth changes, earthquakes, etc. The records do not show any more now than is usual for these occurrences. People who are leaning toward instability are more easily affected by the information than those who are centered in spiritual experiences.

Most of the changes that psychics, etc., are presently reading are changes that are taking place inside of each person. Some of them exteriorize what they perceive and become frightened of what they are seeing in their visualization, and they talk about it and magnify the visualization, etc. We are here to solidify this part of God's creation. So we hold firm and steady and this quells the earthquakes and other earth changes. They will still take place, but not with the ferocity projected by others. We are to dispel the doom and gloom of the end-day soothsayers.

Answers to Life's Questions

Q: Can the upliftment of consciousness lessen the severity of earthquakes and other physical changes?

A: If the consciousness awakens to the love of the Divine and actuates this by expressions of consideration and care (to each other and this planet), then, yes, nature can be positively affected. When the consciousness uplifts sufficiently and people act out of empathy rather than greed, human beings will cease to do those thing that bring imbalance to the natural conditions. Earthquakes and other physical changes are but balancing actions.

Q: My area is experiencing a long drought and forest fires are a problem. We desperately need rain. Is there anything I can do to assist spiritually?

A: It's fine to send the Light to the areas concerned. You might also silently send the tone into the atmosphere, for rain for the highest good. This would be done separate from your personal "s.e. time." If there are other initiates or ministers in your area, you can do this together, perhaps during a "pray-for-rain day." One way you could go about doing it is to stand together, facing where you want the clouds to mass and have moisture in them for the "raining time." Then silently chant your tone while your arms are outstretched toward the area, while your intention for doing this is kept in mind. Five to fifteen minutes should be ample each time you do this. You can do this as a group or individually when you feel like doing it.

EGO

Q: How does the ego relate to the basic, conscious and high selves? Is it part of the basic self?

A: The ego is somewhat a part of the basic self; the ego comes out of the mind and emotions. Many people have the tendency to think that the ego is "bad" when it's actually the thing that makes you think you're worthwhile, that makes you step out and try new things and reaches out to lift and help others.

Q: Is part of the Traveler's work to redirect the ego of mankind?

A: The Traveler's work is as a guide towards Soul Transcendence. In order to do this, one must gain the awareness of the obstacles and the ability to change them to stepping stones. In the Movement of Spiritual Inner Awareness, the Traveler is an awakener. Then it is up to each initiate to do what it takes to transcend the lower levels, albeit with the Traveler's assistance. Ego is a part of the lower realms and is the enemy of Soul. It is up to each individual to transcend that.

> Q: *Is it egotistical to be concerned with my physical appearance?*

A: First of all, there is nothing wrong with ego. Hair styles, dress styles, etc., are all part of this level, and there is nothing wrong with these things as long as you stay free within this level; it's a game that can be fun.

EMOTIONS

> Q: *What is the difference between feelings and emotions?*

A: Feelings are just information. Below the feelings, which are not negative, are the emotions. There is no intellect in the emotions—they are just energy in motion. Often the difficulty is in not directing this energy in an uplifting way, so we may find ourselves expressing anger, hostility, hysteria, and so forth. That's not bad—it just may not be what you want to express.

Energy

Q: When I'm around certain people, I feel as if energy is being drained out of me from my navel area. What can I do about this? Does this phenomenon have anything to do with the vampire legends?

A: To protect yourself against this draining of energy, you can picture in your imagination a white light that is like cheesecloth. In your imagination, start building layer upon layer of this light around your body, especially your torso. You can do this periodically throughout the day to build up the Light around you and to keep it there. After a while, you'll probably be able to build up the layers faster. There's more information on how to do this, and other protective techniques, in *Psychic Protection*.[2] You can also put aluminum foil over your stomach area for protection. In a pinch, if you're sitting on a sofa with loose pillows on it, you could—casually—take one of the small pillows and hold it over your midsection. All these things can help.

The most important thing to remember is to call in the Light and ask it to surround and protect you. You

---

2. *Psychic Protection* by John-Roger is available in bookstores and through MSIA, P.O. Box 513935, Los Angeles, CA 90051, (323) 737-4055.

can also ask the Light for the highest good to go to the person you feel is draining your energy. Then, if they "pull" energy, they could be getting something really nice, and you are less likely to feel drained.

Enlightenment/Illumination

Q: Most religious systems or philosophies seem to be aiming for certain goals and the question of enlightenment seems to be one that is often mentioned. What is enlightenment?

A: I think I can answer the question if I relate it to another word—illumination. Illumination is when we are fulfilled in all of our levels; we have total knowing and beingness. Enlightenment is a position relative to some other point. For example, if you are watching someone do a calculus problem and you don't understand it the first time, we would say that you are ignorant or, in darkness. But the second time it's explained, if you get it, you are enlightened. That is a form of enlightenment. But illumination would be, if someone started to explain the problem and you could just rattle off the whole solution, because you could see where he was going with it without ever being told. Does that make sense to you? Enlightenment has reference to a relative degree or a relationship to some arbitrary point. Illumination is the total fulfillment of all beingness. There are many enlightened people on the planet, but there are not very many who are illuminated.

Focus

Q: I have been reading a lot lately about the power of the subconscious mind and the power of thought. Exactly what is the power of thought and how important is thought in the "scheme of things?"

A: The best way to answer that is to tell you "energy follows thought." That means if you are thinking about hot fudge sundae, all the levels of your consciousness come in line to bring that to you. The same is true for envisioning and moving toward higher awareness and Soul Transcendence. All of you will start making that happen. You will receive cooperation from your mind, emotions, basic selves—and even your subconscious will be guiding you, though you will not be consciously aware of that level. That's why it becomes so important to watch our thoughts because we will create in a physical way those things we have thought about. Also, be careful what you say. Listen to what you say and be sure it represents what you really want in your life.

Forgiveness

Q: I have a sense that I need to keep forgiving myself everything, and it seems to be a great blessing to do that. Do you have any comments on this?

A: Just keep in a state of forgiveness, which is a state of grace. You will not finish up the forgiving until your last breath. A lot of the things that we have remembered keep us here, and we can't get rid of them until we're through with our work here, that is, when we die. In that last moment, the forgiveness will be, "I forgive myself for this," and then the name of God will be the next thing you utter.

Giving & Receiving

Q: It's very easy for me to give and give, but much more difficult for me to receive. How can I learn to receive?

A: You must be open to receive. If I have something to give you but your hands are tightly closed and clenched behind your back, I have no vessel in which to place my gift. But if your hands are open and you reach out to receive, I can place the gift in them.

The same is true for those things that are of Spirit. If you are uptight and closed down inside of yourself, how can you be open to receive the bounty that is available to you?

If it's truly difficult for you to receive, you might begin by receiving in small ways. Let someone buy your lunch, open the door, or run an errand for you. Most people will be very willing to give to you. It's you who decides how much you want to receive on all levels.

Health

Q: How does diet affect spirituality?

A: Let me answer this way: it matters very little what you eat or how much you eat or if you fast or if you drink only liquids or any other diet variation. These are physical patterns that do not determine whether or not you will see the face of God. If one type of diet makes you feel more comfortable than another while you are on your way to God, then it is working for you and it's the one to follow. If you find out that it ceases to work for you, if it begins to look like a detour or a maze with a dead end, then it is no longer working for you and it is probably time to change. Only you can know for sure what is and is not working for you. Let that be your guide.

House Blessing

Q: How would be a good way to bless a new home?

A: If "new" means having been previously occupied but new to you, and you sense that you would like to have a higher energy of Spirit there than was there before, then I would suggest sitting down with the immediate people of concern, which would be the spouse and the children and anyone else who would be living there. I would suggest asking the consciousness that you are following spiritually to come in and clear and cleanse the place. And I would ask that only one consciousness—the consciousness of God—be there. I would ask that anything that is not of that consciousness be removed to wherever it should be removed to according to spiritual dictum.

If it's a brand new home, and if you're living in a rather high state of consciousness, all you have to do is walk through it and say, "God bless this house" and it's blessed. If somebody has died on the construction job, you'd better find that out because they may still be hanging around. And then you may need someone to go in and pick up the consciousness that is earthbound and awaken it so it can move on. It's not doing you any harm; it just feels a little disturbing, that's all.

You can also ask fellow initiates or ministers in MSIA to gather in your home and bless your home and all who enter. In this way, you are opening to receive loving, blessings and fellowship, and you are giving those who love you an opportunity to share that loving with you.

Inner Guidance

Q: What is the difference between the high self and the Inner Master, and the Traveler within?

A: The Mystical Traveler Consciousness is a guide toward Soul Transcendence, and resides on all levels, including the Soul realm. The high self resides below the Soul realm for the purpose of holding the divine guidelines for your karmic lifetime. What you call "the Inner Master" might be the Traveler, or the high self, or a guardian angel. If any inner voice tells you to do something, check it out before doing it. The criteria is not which being is offering what, but rather the nature of the directive. Some have used their inner directives for their physical health (cutting down on caffeine and sugar intake), others for spiritual advancement (greater commitment in service), and others have tried to manipulate their so-called "Inner Master" and have "heard" approval of lustful and/or acquisitive expressions.

I suggest you continue tuning your inner ear by spiritual exercises, expressions of service, study of Soul Awareness Discourses, and participation with people who have committed their lives to the expression of loving and integrity. In time, you will know that your Inner Master or high self or the Traveler is the one offering information for your highest good. The title of the messenger is not nearly as important as the content of the message.

Intuition

Q: I seem to be fairly smart intellectually, but I'm often "off" or "missing" when it comes to "gut level" knowing. How can I increase my gut-level intuitive knowing?

A That type of knowledge comes with time and patience. Experiment with your intuition and then check out how accurate it has been. It may look like a process of watching or trial and error. You may want to test your ability with those people who you know will support and love you and with whom you feel safe. As you feel better about yourself and are less concerned about what other people think about you, you become more aware of your own sense of self. You can then tune in the "true self" anytime you want. Just relax and gain confidence in yourself.

KARMA

Q: Could you explain karma?

A: Karma means action, movement, and at times, the inability to change. It has to do with cause and effect. Because of an action, there is an effect, which is another action. And because of that effect there is another cause. And so on. You are the cause, the effect, and the cause. To stop that pattern, you must stop the effect—the reaction to the cause. You must consciously direct and control your actions, so that you are causing only patterns of Light and love and fulfillment to occur. As you stop all the negative effects, you will break free of the incarnation pattern.

Q: How can I learn to handle karma without having to go through it physically?

A: As long as you are in a physical body, you will have physical karma. Don't curse it, don't try and avoid it or judge it. Bless it, because that is what's keeping you on this planet long enough to learn your divine lessons, eventually enabling you to go home—to Soul, to God. Of course, there are incidents where there are spiritual events transcending and transmuting physical karma. These are sometimes called grace. Other times, those working with the Traveler Consciousness will often work out various levels of karma during spiritual exercises, in night travel while sleeping and dreaming, and in release during acts of service.

Q: Can physical exercise help me move through my karma more quickly, keep my inner environment clean and help me prepare (along with spiritual exercises, of course) for my next initiation?

A: One of the great values of physical exercise is that it calls for discipline. As you learn the joys of discipline, you will then be able to focus on the positive more often and transcend your emotional responses more easily. Such a positive, consistent focus can help you "move through karma" toward your next initiation.

LIGHT

Q: What is the Light? And how do we call it in and work with it?

A: First of all, let me go backwards and say that we all are the Light, automatically. So we really don't have to go too much further than that. We all have a Light within us—it is the Soul; it is that spark of God, of the Divine, that activates our consciousness. That Light, for many reasons, may appear subdued. Then there are the more conscious bearers of Light who bring the Light very strongly into the planet. They will come together in groups and converse about the Light consciousness. They will point up certain universal truths that will awaken the consciousness of people. In the Movement of Spiritual Inner Awareness, this Light form becomes established very rapidly through a pure channel of consciousness. Then all we do is assert the channel of consciousness of our highest good. It cannot form anything other than that. And, of course, there are many techniques of how to do that. But, for the most part, we bring the Light in by asking, "If this be for my highest good and for theirs, then I would like the Light to be placed with me and with them and with our situation or relationship." And remember, Light means Living In God's Holy Thoughts.

Answers to Life's Questions

Q: Lately, I have heard you recommend that we "call ourselves forward to the Light" as opposed to "calling in the Light." What is the difference?

A: The Light is already here. It never leaves us. By calling ourselves forward to the Light, we are acknowledging that and stating what the process is. We are saying, in effect, "I know You are always here, God, and I am consciously bringing myself into Your presence now, so that I can have a fuller knowledge and experience of You."

Q: If all things are happening according to the highest good and in perfect timing, why send the Light?

A: Because Spirit will not usually look at a plan to see if an alternate can be instituted unless requested from this level of Spirit. In the cosmic sense, taking all eternity into consideration, all things are ultimately for the highest good because not one Soul will be lost. But very few of us function at that cosmic, ultimate level. On this level, where most of us function, all things don't seem to necessarily happen for the highest good or in perfect timing. So it's always appropriate to send the Light for the highest good (which is something God knows and we, on our personality levels, don't always know). Sending the Light for the highest good increases the positive energy in a situation and increases the likelihood that, rather than a not-so-high good, the highest good possible will take place.

Q: How long is it effective to pray for someone? Is it valuable for them even after they have passed from the physical world?

A: Praying for someone (or putting them in the Light) is a beautiful expression. If I made any generalization, it might be to do it until it is effective. In time, with enough practice, you will know when your prayers are effective. Effective in terms of the highest good, not necessarily for what you may want. The greatest prayer is: "Thy will be done" (on earth as in heaven).

Q: Is reviewing the MSIA Prayer List before doing s.e.'s valuable?

A: It'd be a good time to do that with s.e.'s, but it's probably already gone by the time you look at it to do s.e.'s. Maybe when you come out of s.e.'s, review the list again. Sending the Light is a form of prayer that's very powerful. We're doing it as a straight, direct contact with God, instead of interceding and using ourselves to explain everything to God, which dilutes the energy. If you just look at the page and say, "Light," that's direct contact. I think that would be a very good thing to do.

Q: I spend much of my day commuting on a bus or a bicycle. Can I successfully plant Light columns while traveling on these vehicles?

A: You can, and that's an excellent idea.

Q: Can I place a Light column somewhere when my physical body is not there to anchor it physically?

A: You can send the Light to anyone or anyplace; however, to place a Light column that will withstand the energy of negative forces for a lengthy period of time, it is more effective when you anchor it physically.

Q: What is the best way to let people know about the Light and the Traveler?

A: The best way to spread the Light is to live the Light and be the Light in all your actions and expressions.

Talking about the Light can sometimes be the poorest way to communicate, since words can so often be misrepresentations of the truth and be misinterpreted by the listener. People can and do receive benefit from the loving that you extend out to them, and some will "catch the Spirit" and ask you what you have that seems so loving. You can then say, "I'm glad you asked," and tell them of your personal experience with the Light. The ones who are to consciously work with the Light and the Traveler will touch to it when the time is right and they are ready.

Love

Q: It seems like the happier and the more loving I get, the more people pick on me and tell me I'm wrong. I don't think I am, but it's getting harder to be with some people. And sometimes I react, and then I don't demonstrate loving. What can I do?

A: There will be people, God bless them, who will hate you for doing all the things that demonstrate loving of yourself because it also demonstrates to them that they are not doing that for themselves. Instead of them learning that they can also be loving, they will try to castigate you and prove you wrong—and they can. They'll hit your car, hit you, pick on your family, and if you explode and try to get back at them, they will say, "See, you weren't living your teachings." But life is like that. If that happens, you just immediately go right back into the teachings again. You're allowed all sorts of mistakes in learning anything. None of us came in with this level perfected. There is a rightness and properness that takes place spiritually, however, and that's where we want to keep the focus.

Q: I feel a lot of love in my heart for people, but I have a really difficult time expressing that out into the world. I keep a lot of it bottled up inside me, and I just don't tell people how I'm feeling.

A: If you have the love in your heart, that's the most important thing, and you can communicate and express that love in silent ways. You can send the Light to people. You can send them your love. You can support them and understand them in what they do—silently, if you haven't yet done that outwardly.

As you continue to do that, you'll find that it starts "showing" and other people will become aware of that. They just might see it in the smile in your eyes. They might sense it in your silence. People are really good at picking up when someone loves them. So don't worry about expressing it outwardly. Just keep the love flowing in your heart and you'll be fine.

Q: How do you put up with all this?

A: Without love, there isn't a chance.

Q: Do you have anything to share with me for my highest good?

A: Love yourself, love your family, love others, love life, love all things—and do your s.e.'s to become more aware of God's great love for you.

Q: Who was Melchizedek and what is his relationship to MSIA? Where can I learn more about this great Soul?

A: Melchizedek was a high priest during the time of Abraham who established the priesthood of unconditional loving. MSIA ministers are ordained into the Melchizedek line of energy. Melchizedek also introduced the concept of tithing as an expression of recognition that all things come from God.

Prior to Melchizedek, the priesthood was called the Order of the Priesthood of the Son of God. Perhaps if you go to a library section with comprehensive esoteric teachings, you might find more about this magnificent Soul of God.

Answers to Life's Questions

Mystical Traveler

Q: Could you explain to me how the Traveler works?

A: It's important to remember that the Traveler is not something separate from you. It's a consciousness that is within each person on all levels: the imagination, the mind, the emotions, the unconscious, the Soul, and the Spirit. Each person's inner spiritual journey is an awakening to the Traveler on all the levels, up into the very heart of God. For more information about how this loving consciousness assists people, I highly recommend the seminar, "When the Mystical Traveler Works with You."

Q: Is there a way that we individually or as a group can assist your body to be healthier, other than sending the Light? Would seeding help in this case?

A: What might assist is that when people ask for the Traveler's help, they ask for the Spirit part of the Traveler to help and they focus on that. Too many people focus on the physical part of the Traveler, and then it tends to interrupt the flow of energy to my body. This is how I end up "eating" most of what I "eat" for others. So, it would help a lot to focus on the Spirit part, not the physical part, and then I can do it from the Spirit, not the physical.

> *Q: What happens when the physical body for the Traveler dies? What is the next step for the students of that Traveler? Do the students of the Traveler who died continue to maintain any connection with him?*

A: Actually, the body of the one who has fully awakened to the Mystical Traveler Consciousness has no students. However, you can study the teachings which originate from a bodyless source. Yes, the divine energy of the Mystical Traveler Consciousness has always been present on the earth, working through a human being. Although there have been many times when the particular human being was not known as a Mystical Traveler Consciousness, the spiritual energy of the Traveler was nonetheless effective according to the particular spiritual man. (Each Mystical Traveler Consciousness does not always have the same mission, although all Travelers channel divinity from the same source.)

If you embrace the teachings and techniques offered through the Traveler Consciousness, you can then recognize that during your spiritual exercises you can be in contact with the Mystical Traveler Consciousness which is within you. During your inner journey to the higher realms, the experience has little to do with the physical body of the one who has awakened fully to the Mystical Consciousness.

If God's plan is to continue the spiritual history of the Mystical Traveler Consciousness on this planet, when the body of one dies, the consciousness will be present in another. Will you know who that is? Some will, some won't. For those who continue to do their spiritual exercises and expressions of service in devotion, it may not matter.

Ministry

Q: How can I answer when someone asks me what being a minister in MSIA is all about?

A: Maybe we shouldn't look upon ourselves so much as ministers but as facilitators or people who assist other people. Our function is more that of facilitating and not evangelizing, proselytizing, or necessarily witnessing to anything the way some ministers in other churches do. Instead, it is much like how a doctor would minister or a Boy Scout or Girl Scout. In other words, it is more the level of giving assistance.

For the most part, I wouldn't play myself up to be a minister of anything. A person is likely to have problems with others over his or her ministry only when the person stands up and announces, "I'm Reverend So-and-So from the Church of the Movement of Spiritual Inner Awareness." Instead of doing that, let your assistance and your service speak for themselves.

NAMES OF GOD

Q: Could you clarify what is meant by the 108 names of God?

A: Since human beings awakened to the knowledge of God, they have had a need to give that omnipotent energy a name.

There are at least 108 names that assimilate into the loving energy of God. If you say any of those 108 names without the essence of loving, you are not attuning to that particular frequency, and you will not experience God. If you come from your unconditionally loving center, attuned to the frequency of giving in God, the name isn't that important. Shakespeare wrote, "A rose by any other name would smell as sweet."

Answers to Life's Questions

Peace

Q: Is peace in our genetic code?

A: The potential for peace is in the human genetic code, but it is not activated in many people. It is being activated in those who are moving into a higher consciousness, which includes peace.

Q: I've heard the phrase, "Let there be peace, and let it begin with me." Do you have any suggestions for getting some peace going inside myself?

A: I'll answer that with a little story. When Prana first got started, the people there would sometimes stay up all night doing mailings. They would wonder how they were going to get up and go to work the next day, but they didn't have to worry; they never got a chance to go to bed. They just went to work the next day and worked beautifully and life was wonderful and it just happened to be one of those longer days. Spirit met them at their point of physical action. They were truly being of service, not as a reward action or something done for recognition, but as a loving action that comes from the heart.

When that comes forward, this Mother-Father-God comes forward in you and starts to perform the action of your work through your beingness. You find it effortless. You find it going better than you thought it was going to go. You even wonder if you're missing something—everything gets done so quickly. But you find out, no, everything is done.

We are here to learn one thing primarily, and that's inner peace. In the midst of all else, when you put your body on the line, and get your actions lined up with your loving, you can start to experience this inner peace. This was a long way around to make a point, but I think you got the message.

> Q: *I feel very peaceful and calm and relaxed in some places, even if that's not how I felt when I first got there. But I've heard that I shouldn't need an outer reference point for feeling calm and peaceful that I should be able to create that from inside myself no matter where I am. Am I doing something wrong?*

A: You may be particularly sensitive to the energy around you, which may mean that when you are in an area full of a lot of different people's thoughts and emotions, you are aware of them on some level and they may be disturbing to you. When you are in an area that is full of devic energy, or perhaps where people have done spiritual exercises, you may feel more at peace because there is less disturbance in the energy field of that area.

One thing you can do is to start anchoring your experience of the calm places into your consciousness. One way to do that is to create a signal to yourself while you are feeling the peace and calm. You might touch certain fingers together, or tap a place on your arm, or whatever is simple and easy for you to do. Then, when you are in an area of greater turmoil and confusion, you can use your signal to activate the memory of the calm. This may take repetition and practice, but it can be helpful.

You can always call in the Light wherever you are, and place Light columns for the highest good. You may be in a process of strengthening your consciousness so that you can hold a place of peace and Light regardless of what is going on around you. And it may sometimes be best for you to remove yourself physically from an area where the energy is too disturbing to you. You will know what is right for you.

SERVICE

Q: In other answers you have given, you've said service is a way of handling the 10-percent level. Does this work in the same way spiritual exercises do?

A: No. I have said that service is the highest expression on this physical level. That is giving for the joy of giving, with no recompense. One of the great values of service is the alignment a person can have, on the physical level, with the energy of Spirit.

Spiritual exercises are not an expression intended for this physical level. S.e.'s are, in fact, the exercises that allow the consciousness to transcend the physical, and awaken to the glory of Spirit in the higher realms.

Q: I know I have a lot of love inside me, and I want to do something that will make a difference in the world. Do you have any suggestions?

A: Loving, caring, and sharing—these words are spelled with an "ing" on the end. Not love, but loving. Get out there and scratch your spouse's back when it itches. Get out there and work with the people around you when they need help. Put your body out there doing what's there to be done, and keep your attitude clean, where you don't judge the action of what's going on around you—that's caring. Sharing is a by-product of all that. I've come to the conclusion that the highest form of consciousness that we can manifest physically is service to humanity. That serving doesn't have to have anything worthwhile to serve. It just serves willingly, openly, lovingly, caringly. Then a contentment can just appear, where you're content with you, with the Lord in you and everything is just OK with you. I hope that answers your question.

Silent Ones

Q: Who are the Silent Ones?

A: The Silent Ones are masters who are here to serve silently. These beings have the ability to take many forms and whose job it is to teach and test you. An example might be a bum on skid row; when you see him you have an aversion to his outer appearance and apparent circumstances. He might be there to teach you unconditional love or total acceptance. The safest territory you can be in is to stay in your loving heart as much as possible and not let the fear of running into a Silent One run you. When you are truly in that centered and loving place, all tests are passed with ease. It's called practice, practice, practice.

When you meet one of those Silent Ones (and only you know where your weaknesses lie) use it to your advantage to grow and lift yourself into new awarenesses. Then go on to the next situation. Awareness is such a key in all of our lives. There is so much more that could be said about the Silent Ones—for instance: they run creation.

Sound Current

Q: Why is the Sound Current not mentioned in the Bible?

A: The Sound Current is mentioned in the Bible. It is spoken of as the "Word made flesh." You will also see it referred to as, "the wind blows wherever it pleases. You hear its sound but you cannot tell where it comes from or where it is going."[3] If you read your Bible in awareness, you will be surprised how many references there are to the Sound Current.

---

3. St. John 3:8, New International Version

Answers to Life's Questions

Spiritual Exercises

Q: Sometimes during the day, I feel a beautiful close connection to the Traveler and to God. Are these experiences of connection a form of spiritual exercises?

A: They are the best times. After one does s.e.'s, the next step is a "living relationship," as you have described. At some point, we have to stop doing s.e.'s and start walking with the Lord.

Q: Is doing my spiritual exercises being of service?

A: There's a place in the Bible where it says, "God loves a joyful giver." So when you give the two hours joyfully and go inside and do your spiritual exercises, there's a real payoff inside. The emphasis of giving has been out here into the world, and it's true that "when you've done it to the least of these, you've done it unto me." But God also loves one who gives back inside, where you give to the God inside of you, and that's called Baruch Hashem, "Praise the Lord." When you do your spiritual exercises, have that attitude of living in the praises of joy. That'll bring forward the spiritual energy of the s.e.'s real fast, and then you can ride on your tone back inside.

Stubbornness & Perseverance

Q: How can I know the difference between being stubborn or persevering in order to reach a goal?

A: This takes a lot of discernment and practice. It takes asking for guidance, listening, and being willing to follow the way that Spirit is leading. Most of the time, stubbornness has resistance in it. Persevering has a clear direction.

Q: What is the difference between stubbornness and will?

A: Stubbornness is an automatic reaction. Will is a choice. However, stubbornness usually follows through with the choice as an automatic reaction. Long after you've stopped choosing, it may still carry on with the choice, because it hasn't received a new direction from you.

Stubbornness used the right way becomes determination. Instead of holding back, it then reaches out and pulls. Stubbornness is akin to grief, a form of sadness, of futility, of hopelessness, of loss, where determination is one of hope, of youth, of life, of vitality. Knowing those and putting them in your attitude starts to change the flow of energy.

ANSWERS TO LIFE'S QUESTIONS

10–PERCENT & THE TRAVELER

Q: I am new to MSIA and have recently heard you say that the Traveler works in the 90 percent and that we have to work the 10 percent. What do you mean by that?

A: I work through the spiritual realms to strengthen the Soul and to increase the awareness of Soul consciousness until you become capable of establishing yourself on the Soul realm. I work only for your highest good and assist you in your working through your karmic path. It is important that you complete your life pattern according to the plan you set out for yourself before this incarnation. It is important for you to take responsibility for the decisions of your life and the path that you chose to travel. Physical-level problems (10-percent level) or situations are your opportunities for greater growth and upliftment. Your choices are left to your discretion so that you will grow in wisdom and awareness and so that you will fulfill your life plan the way that is right and proper for you. As long as you do not hurt yourself or others, what you do or do not do physically makes very little difference in the spiritual work that I do with you.

TRUST

Q: How do you know if you can trust someone?

A: You can't actually "trust" anyone; you can love everyone as you love yourself. One of the greatest challenges we have is to love ourselves unconditionally. Loving generally is a process of going inward, and trusting generally is a process of going outside yourself to another person—trying to find what you think is lacking in yourself. In personal and business matters, build your foundation slowly with those people you associate with. Don't sell yourself short and let them earn your respect. But give your love abundantly!

Baruch Bashan
The Blessings Already Are

SELECTED BIBLIOGRAPHY

The following books and materials can support you in learning more about the ideas presented in Answers to Life's Questions. They can be ordered through the Movement of Spiritual Inner Awareness at: 800-899-2665, www.msia.org, order@msia.org

Audio and Video Albums

Some items are available in audio format only (CDs), while others are available in both audio and video (DVDs). Items listed with "SAT" next to the catalog number are part of the Soul Awareness Tapes series (now on CDs), which are selected audio recordings of John-Roger seminars, meditations, and sharings that are sent each month to SAT subscribers. Once you subscribe, you can also obtain previously issued SAT selections. Please note that some of the CDs in this Bibliography are part of the SAT series, and you would need to be a subscriber to receive them.

Audio and Video Materials

Approaching God Through Grace (#7420-CD, SAT)

Are You Doing God's Will? (#7674-CD, SAT)

Awakening to the Mystical Traveler Consciousness (#2017-CD)

Basic Instructions for Spiritual Exercises (#7535-CD, SAT)

Answers to Life's Questions

Cathedral of the Soul (#3714-CD)

Changing Your Behavior to a Spiritual Nature (#7594-CD, SAT)

Chanting the Sacred Tones (#7001-CD, Spanish/English)

Discourses and the Value of Introspection (#7234-CD)

God is Intention (#7354-CD, #7354-DVD)

Guidance Into the Heart of God (#7557-CD, SAT)

Initiation—Molding the Golden Chalice (#2601-CD)

Inner Journey Through Spirit Realms (#7251-CD)

Innerphasing for Multidimensional Consciousness (#7694-CD)

Mystical Traveler: Direct Line to God (#7127-CD, #7127-DVD)

Passages to the Realms of Spirit (#7037-CD, #7037-DVD)

Psychic Violence (#7308-CD, #7308-DVD)

Sound Current (#2021-CD)

Soul Realm Mock-up and Beyond (#7459-CD, SAT)

Stalking the Spirit (#7347-CD, #7347-DVD)

Twelve Approaches to Spirituality (#2619-CD, SAT)

Upgrading Our Addictions to God (#7487-CD, SAT)

What is the Blessing of Soul Transcendence?
  (#1131-CD, SAT)

When the Mystical Traveler Works with You
  (#2053-CD)

Worship God with Your Soul
  (#7476-CD, SAT)

CD Sets

The Anointed One, (Three CD set, #3906-CD)

Inner Worlds of Meditation (Three CD set, #3915-CD)

Living in Grace (Four CD set, #3903-CD)

Spiritual Warrior (Five CD set, #3905-CD)

The Wayshower (Four CD set with booklet,
  #3901-CD)

Books

Available at bookstores everywhere, and through MSIA

Forgiveness, The Key to the Kingdom (#0914829629)

Inner Worlds of Meditation (#0914829459)

Loving Each Day (#0914829262)

Spiritual Warrior: The Art of Spiritual Living
   (#01482936X)

The Tao of Spirit (#0914829335)

For additional study materials, please visit our online store at www.msia.org

To order, contact the Movement of Spiritual Inner Awareness at 800-899-2665, or order@msia.org, or simply visit our online store.

SOUL AWARENESS DISCOURSES

Soul Awareness Discourses are designed to teach Soul Transcendence, which is becoming aware of yourself as a Soul and as one with God, not as a theory, but as a living reality. They are for people who want a consistent, time-proven approach to their spiritual unfoldment.

A set of Soul Awareness Discourses consists of 12 booklets, one to study and contemplate each month of the year. As you read each Discourse, you can activate an awareness of your Divine essence and deepen your relationship with God.

Spiritual in essence, Discourses are compatible with religious beliefs you might hold. In fact, most people find that Discourses support the experience of whatever path, philosophy, or religion (if any) they choose to follow. Simply put, Discourses are about eternal truths and the wisdom of the heart.

The first year of Discourses addresses topics ranging from creating success in the world to working hand-in-hand with Spirit.

A yearly set of Discourses is regularly $100. MSIA is offering the first year of Discourses at an introductory price of $50. Discourses come with a full, no-questions-asked, money-back guarantee. If at any time you decide this course of study is not right for you, simply return it, and you will promptly receive a full refund.

To order Discourses, contact the Movement of Spiritual Inner Awareness at 1-800-899-2665, order@msia.org, or visit www.msia.org

Soul Awareness Tape (SAT) Series (now on CDs)

Subscription to the SAT series provides a new seminar by John-Roger each month, on a variety of topics ranging from practical living to spiritual upliftment. In addition, the entire SAT library of hundreds of seminars and meditations is available to SAT subscribers.

The New Day Herald

A bi-monthly publication which includes articles by John-Roger as well as informative pieces and a calendar of events around the world sponsored by The Movement of Spiritual Inner Awareness and Peace Theological Seminary & College of Philosophy.

A one-year subscription is free upon request. You can also subscribe to the free electronic version at www.newdayherald.org

LOVING EACH DAY

Loving Each Day is a daily e-mail message that contains an uplifting quote or passage from John-Roger or John Morton. These messages are intended to inspire you and give you pause to reflect on the Spirit within. Loving Each Day is available in four languages: English, Spanish, French and Portuguese.

A subscription is free upon request. To subscribe, please visit the web site www.lovingeachday.org.

CDs, DVDs, books and subscriptions are available from MSIA at the address below. We welcome your comments and questions. Please contact us at:

MSIA
P.O. Box 513935
Los Angeles, CA 90051-1935
323-737-4055
FAX 323-737-5680
soul@msia.org
www.msia.org

Books by John-Roger are available at bookstores everywhere.

John-Roger, DSS

A teacher and lecturer of international stature, John-Roger is an inspiration in the lives of many people around the world. For over four decades, his wisdom, humor, common sense and love have helped people to discover the Spirit within themselves and find health, peace, and prosperity.

With two co-authored books on the New York Times Bestseller list to his credit, and more than three dozen spiritual and self-help books and audio albums, John-Roger offers extraordinary insights on a wide range of topics. He is the founder of the Church of the Movement of Spiritual Inner Awareness (MSIA), which focuses on Soul Transcendence; founder and Chancellor of the University of Santa Monica; founder and President of Peace Theological Seminary & College of Philosophy; founder and chairman of the board of Insight Seminars; and founder and President of The Institute for Individual & World Peace.

John-Roger has given over 6,000 lectures and seminars worldwide, many of which are televised nationally on his cable program, "That Which Is," through the Network of Wisdoms. He has appeared on numerous radio and television shows and been a featured guest on "Larry King Live."

An educator and minister by profession, John-Roger continues to transform lives by educating people in the wisdom of the spiritual heart.

For more information about John-Roger, you may also visit:

www.john-roger.org

Breinigsville, PA USA
15 June 2010
239920BV00001B/11/A